Other Books by Carol Lynn Stevenson Grellas

Alice in Ruby Slippers, Kelsay Books
Hasty Notes in No Particular Order, Kelsay Books (Aldrich Press)
Things I Can't Remember to Forget, Prolific Press
On the Edge of the Ethereal, Kelsay Books
The Nightly Suicides, Kattywompus Press
Letters Under the Banyan Tree, Kelsay Books (Aldrich Press)
In the Making of Goodbyes, Clare Songbirds Publishing House
An Ode to Hope in the Midst of Pandemonium, Main Street Rag
Epitaph for the Beloved, Finishing Line Press
The Wanderer's Dominion, Kelsay Books

(The books listed below are out of print but available upon request)

Epistemology of an Odd Girl, March Street Press
A Thousand Tiny Sorrows, March Street Press
Breakfast in Winter, Flutter Press
Litany of Finger Prayers, Pudding House Press
Object of Desire, Finishing Line Press
The Butterfly Room, Big Table Publishing
Before I Go to Sleep, Red Ochre Press
Desired Things, e-chap, Gold Wake Press

HANDFUL OF STALLIONS AT TWILIGHT

poems by

Carol Lynn Stevenson Grellas

Finishing Line Press
Georgetown, Kentucky

HANDFUL OF STALLIONS AT TWILIGHT

For my husband, who waited patiently while I followed my dream and went back to school to get my MFA in Poetry. I am forever grateful.

A special thank you to my Saturday Writing Workshop, Stan Zumbiel, Linda Collins, Rick Rayburn, Susan Flynn, Bob Stanley, Lynn Belzer, and Connie Gutowsky, all of whom have read first drafts of several of these poems.

Copyright © 2024 by Carol Lynn Stevenson Grellas
ISBN 979-8-88838-585-2 First Edition
All rights reserved under International and Pan-American Copyright Conventions. No part of this book may be reproduced in any manner whatsoever without written permission from the publisher, except in the case of brief quotations embodied in critical articles and reviews.

Publisher: Leah Huete de Maines
Editor: Christen Kincaid
Cover Art: The Tower of Blue Horses Franz Marc—Zenodot Verlagsgesellschaft mbH and licensed under the GNU Free Documentation License.
Author Photo: David & Ally McKay, McKay Photography
Cover Design: Elizabeth Maines McCleavy

Order online: www.finishinglinepress.com
also available on amazon.com

Author inquiries and mail orders:
Finishing Line Press
PO Box 1626
Georgetown, Kentucky 40324
USA

Contents

If My Death Could Be a Whale Fall 1
Before Tomorrow Came 2
When I Think of You 3
Just Another Ending 5
Clemency and the Green House 7
Imagine 8
Cinders 9
The Father-Daughter Dialogues 11
A Mother's Daughter 13
After Admiring a Vintage Portrait in an Antique Store 14
Leap Year 16
Eleven Pipers Piping 17
Aunt Susan 19
Old Painting That Hangs in My House 20
Save Our Souls 21
In the Line at Starbucks 22
When You're Small, and Your Father Won't Wake Up 23
On the Occasion of Your Mother's Hip Replacement 25
Down by the Watershed 26
Negotiations Between Things with Plumage 28
After Eating Candy at the Matinee 29
For the Boy Who Swam at Midnight 30
For the Lost Child 32
Shadows in the Moonlight 33
Audrie's Poem 35
Minutes from My Doctor's Appointment after My Parents Died. 36
Cigars, Cigarettes, and Me 38
The Boyfriend? 39
In Another Life 40
Homage to this Heart 41
Tiny Mercies 42
Terms of Endearment and a Grandmother's Word 44
Regarding Your Submission 46
To the Editor Who Knew Me from My Poems 48
Cat Remembers Being Young 50
Listen, Darling 52

Dear Penny's Lingerie Police..54
The Day I was a Visiting 2nd Grade Teacher...55
The Haunting 56
Excavation of an Expired Womb..58
Song Dynasty 60
How to Fall in Love with Robert Bly...61
Handful of Stallions at Twilight..63
Rage at My Father's Illness 65
When an Interruption in Your Contentment Takes Place 66
Memo to My Children...68
Epistolary Thoughts from an Aging Schoolgirl.....................................69
The Gingham Dress..70
When Last That Sadness Bloomed...72
The Benediction..73
Empty Nester..75
While You Were Having Your Colonoscopy...76
Forgive Me...77
There Is the House..78
I Swallowed Forty Stars...79
An Unexpected Toast...80
Abandoned..81
August Bride...83
An Imagined Life...84

Acknowledgments...86

If My Death Could Be a Whale Fall

I'd like my death to be valued rather than mourned,
like a whale's carcass lying on the ocean floor

a juncture for adaptive radiation. That would make
dying something to be grateful for, my body generating

new life, giving positive meaning to the words *bottom
feeders*, all creatures large and small, who would benefit

from my bones and filaments decomposing in the sea.
My whole self, lying dormant to an invasion of living things

beyond me, my lungs emptied of air, my skeleton bared
to scavengers, a breeding ground of trophic splendor

the way even tiny corpses are named *marine snow*
that shower the waters with sustenance. What if

my remains could be dropped through the sea after my heart
decides to halt its beating, left to decompose, spoil

and crumble organically under a ceremonial term
like *death's rain*. A way to give back to the earth again,

and again and again. What if I could become part
of a legacy for all that feed on the remnants

of what once was? Surely, my soul will wake
and rise from its sunken bed in search of the Divine

as it blooms in effervescence the way
champagne bubbles sparkle and dance

as they float to the rim of a crystal glass, then roll
over the crest onto a thirsty and beautiful tongue.

Before Tomorrow Came

In this pandemic, I'm thankful for the chance
to say *I love you* because there's not
always tomorrow when the world's been thrown

a curveball. Where's Superman when you need
him? I thought I could do it, you know, save
the whole universe, but God must have gotten

annoyed with my prayers after a while. Too much
to handle, so many problems all at once. It can't be
easy being the one who watches over everyone.

I know, just from worrying about my own children.
I have hives in several undisclosed places.
At least my dermatologist says that's what they're

from. An unscientific term she calls *motherly unease*—
my joy and anxiety have always been from
my kids. But now it's only anxiety about mine

and everyone's kids. Still, each night, I set
the table, and I'm grateful for the home we
live in, for the walls that shelter us—

and for the windows that overlook the garden
where we used to walk beneath the gazebo
beside the roses in bloom, where we'd talk

about a wedding planned for June, or who's
wearing what this coming year—and as I place
a glass to the right of each dinner plate

and arrange the Waterford silverware carefully
over double-folded napkins, as I position chairs
for us who used to sit together and enjoy

a meal with banter about the day's doings:
a parking ticket, a college acceptance letter,
a broken washing machine, a visit to the vet,

now I'm just grateful to sit together,
and for memories of what used to be.

When I Think of You

I'm thinking of the Green Jade Flower—
I'm thinking of you and the Green Jade Flower,
and the way I love the warmth of your skin
when you brush against my cheek in moonlight
soft as a petal, kissing me goodnight. I'm thinking
of the Green Jade Flower, with its purplish
buds and evocative claw-like blooms of emerald
and turquoise blue that look like the folded
wings of a butterfly, and the deforestation
that's endangered its dwelling on the Islands
of the Philippines. I'm thinking of the Green
Jade Flower, as if it is you, as if my actions
make a difference in its life,
make a difference in yours—

I'm thinking of the white-tailed deer—
I'm thinking of you and the white-tailed
deer, and the way I love the sound
of your voice in the morning, the way you
say my name in a soothing tone as we sit
together on the patio under a sheltering
of leaves. I'm thinking of the white-tailed deer
with its flared fringed tail, roaming the savanna
woodlands, broadleaf forests, and swamps
hunting for plants exposed to disease,
stochastic happenings while environmental
ruin is hampering its home. I'm thinking
of the white-tailed deer as if it is you, as if
my actions make a difference in its life,
make a difference in yours—

I'm thinking of the polar bear—
I'm thinking of you and the polar bear,
and the way I love the scent of the sea
in your hair after a stroll on the beach
bathed in the glow of afternoon light.
I'm thinking of the polar bear, its luminescent
double coat, the way it travels over
the Arctic Ocean on swathes of moving
ice through wintering nights, its habitat
weakening due to global warming, holes
in the ozone layer and the devastation

its endured. I'm thinking of the polar
bear as if it is you, as if my actions make
a difference in its life, make a difference
in yours—

I'm thinking of the entire planet—
I'm thinking of you, the entire planet,
and the way your face tilts upward
when you smile, your body leaning
into mine, your lungs bartering air
for laughter, how we count on breathing,
sustenance and water to survive.
I'm thinking of the entire planet and the threat
of pollution, climate change, and the misuse
of natural resources as if the entire planet
is you, as if my actions make a difference
in all life, make a difference in yours,
which I believe they do.

Just Another Ending

I remember the night of the *Harvest Moon*,
its September beginning named for schooldays,
the smell of sharpened pencils, the chance
of each new morning after one gaze
into a vast pearl blur. How everything felt
graspable, how I thought I loved the boy
next door with his sweet talk and guitars,
then, one day, he moved away.

I remember the night of the *Wolf Moon*,
the cold frost that tipped tiny leaves
of the stephanotis beneath the arbor
on the front porch of my house as a child—
January days when it rained, the yellow
galoshes I'd leave outside, how little petals
fell like skirts of tulle around the entrance
to our home, drops of floral milk from broken
flowers on the brick patio as though they cried
before they touched the ground, my father
and his Chesterfields, how his firelight
lit the dark when he returned home from Korea,
his mind a warzone, a hunter keeping
predators from our door.

I remember the night of the *Blue Moon*,
and opening my window to the sound of ghosts,
how the darkness felt unending with the ache
of parting, and I thought of my mother
when she died—how everyone left the room
while I remained, death seeming impossible
if I could still hold her hand
and lie beside her.

I remember the night of the *Supermoon*,
the way a stranger pushed me down on
the bed as a lighted glow pressed
against the glass of my window, how I
finally gave up the fight as he entered
my body. I closed my eyes and felt myself
evaporate inside the room, vanish the way
a snail crawls within itself and waits.
No voice can cry for help when a hand
is held over the mouth, but years later,

a beaten bird flew from my throat
like a tiny winged being
finally freed and able to fly.

On the night of the *Blood Moon*,
I remembered all the other nights, how each
memory lived on in search of a better ending.
Hope is almost always hidden as a power
unto itself released into the universe
that awakens me from every moon beyond
my mother's death, beyond my days
of childhood and my father's illness,
beyond my body being violated, beyond
the girl who thought someone could
save her besides herself.

Clemency and the Green House

There's a story in this house, a poem
to be written, this place with a covering
of green paint and brick. Where a woman
grew old with no one to love her,
as she cried past walls and shutter-
dressed windows.

But the house heard her weeping, her
lamenting of days when no one would
answer, her howls long ignored. It wanted
to save her, to make her feel needed,
fill her with hope and remedy her wounds.

Where were the children who named
her a mother, where was the husband
whose pictures were there? She sang
to the house and asked it for comfort,
she sobbed to the house and prayed

on its floors. This house has a story,
a poem to be written, this house with
a covering of green paint and brick.
It opened its doors and let in the birds,
it let in the irises and a fluttering of bees.

And when death was coming, calling
her name, she talked to the house
and begged it to hold her as it
bathed her skin in candlelight breaths.
And the shrubs became lavish,

a vision of beauty, a distraction
like mercy for being alone. And no
one noticed the woman was missing—
just that the house was even more beautiful,
just that the garden was even more lush,

with its shadow of trees in a mournful pose.
But the house remembers, the house
with a story, with a poem to be written,
with a woman still there, her hands
long clenched to a gathering of irises,

dead petals dried in a crown on her head.

Imagine

—for Susan

When I feed the birds, I'm like the old woman
sitting on the steps of the church, my life nearly
over, as if my possessions have been burned

in a fire, and I don't care, as though all that I have
are the birds that come to me, a cluster of pigeons
waiting for seeds, for the echo of my voice carried

in the wind as it rings like a sharp but lonely sound,
the way a chapel bell is both sad and beautiful.
To be nameless among creatures with wings

is to feel cherished by angels, a wanderer among
wanderers where there is no sorrow or weeping
about time gone by, only the soft hum of longing

that fades like rain onto a field of poppies.
Yet the birds are drawn to such loneliness—my palms
upturned in a gesture of giving. They see my offering

as it spills and sparkles through air like a constellation
of falling stars. Tiny messengers of the present,
little scavengers roaming free that wait beside me,

and follow my voice as if I'm some kind of God,
scattering food across stairs. And on these days,
I know what it is to connect with something so precious,

to sense the nowness of time, a wet breeze lifting
my hair as leaves loosen from limbs and drop
to the earth like upside-down moons. On these days

I don't worry about death. I know part of me will live on
in the birds like hope, hunger, or a thirst that's never fully
quenched as they surround me in a moment that feels

otherworldly. And sometimes I hear their song,
a melancholy aria before it disappears into the turbulent
universe. But what I want to tell you is—they are singing

with joy, they are singing *I love you* to anyone who listens.

Cinders

It was only a dream, I tell myself—
a soft glow breaking through a slivered
light beneath the pulled curtain's hem.

My mother again, her ghost interrupting
what should be sleep. This time
she's not in the dream. This time

someone is going through her things,
making piles of giveaways—
maybe the women in the Greek church

will come and collect them,
send her dresses to the poor. Maybe
the neighbors will want her Chanel suit,

her Gucci handbag. I've seen them
watching us from across the street,
all the drama the dying make. Nurses,

and paramedics, the weekly ambulance
rides following rounds of accidents,
my mother walking into mirrors,

unable to focus, unable to even see
her reflection. This is the aftermath
of death, the details left behind, piles

of clothes like dead bodies waiting to be
buried, and I don't want to leave them—
I want to bring them home with me,

carry them through the darkness, my arms
so full I can't see a path to follow.
I want to breathe a Sunday prayer

into the room, into my dream, as if
a tiny bit of life could be restored
one minute more before an inevitable

ending. If I wear the chiffon, maybe
I'll hear her laugh again, if I wear the silk
maybe there'll be petals of daisies

crushed in forgotten pockets, if I wear
her lavender dress, maybe I can run away
from the impending storm, experience

its soft lining rubbing across my heart,
the scent of her perfume wafting in air—
but they've all vanished now, like old

bones burned in a fire, and I'm awake,
with nothing left but the illusiveness
of the dream, like remnants of fading

stars just beyond my window.

The Father-Daughter Dialogues

> "Lewy body dementia is a devastating brain disorder
> ...for which we have no effective treatments."
> —Sonja Scholz, M.D., Ph.D.

My nurse looks like Hitler; I don't want
anti-Semites in this house. You know
I lived in Germany when I was young.
I've got knives hidden beneath the bed;
no one said she'd be sleeping here.
Someone should stay with me—you could
take up in the other room. I've got things
to do tomorrow, so make sure you're here
on time. I don't like waiting. It's not easy
being single at my age. Women are always
asking my name at the temple. I've collected
my loose teeth and laid them on the coverlet;
they're like collectibles. Now you know why
I love banana cream pie. Just like your mother.
Will she be home soon? I just texted Hillary
Clinton and told her she'd have my vote
if she ran again. Next time I walk barefoot
in the moonlight, I won't be pleased if the cops
take me to the hospital. Your uncle is the only
cop I'd trust. It wasn't my fault; some guy
on a motorbike with a yellow sign told me
to drive straight through the barbed-wire fence.
Two deer were standing on the hillside,
their heads bowed, and the silver moonlight
was streaming across the meadow between
them. They looked like angels. They were so
beautiful. I had to leave the car in the middle
of the field. The engine was smoking—
they don't make 'em like they used to!
I prefer hitchhiking now anyway. Is this ID
bracelet really necessary? I know your phone
number by heart. Even if I didn't, you always
find me like you're a sleuth or something.
I can't remember when you're coming over.
You say all the days that end in 'why' (y).
I'm not sure what's real anymore. You shouldn't
have told the people at the synagogue I'm not
really a CIA agent. You know I went to Harvard,

right? I was on a softball team called *The Tortfeasors*.
Next time we visit your mother's grave, let's split
the cost of flowers. Lavender roses, those are still
her favorite. You were always such a good girl,
but you're starting to look your age. There's something
outside the house, red flashing lights.
They've come to take me away. Quick, hide
in the kitchen and bring the dog. By the way,
if you want the piano, it's all yours, but the wheels
need repair. Bear likes to urinate in the living room.
Your grandmother wanted you to have it. It's a vintage
Steinway 1928 player with music rolls. I've marked
the best ones in red ink Good! with an exclamation
point. I'm flying to New York. I've met someone,
so don't try to stop me. My mind's made up. I'll be
gone by morning. I'm tired of this one-trick pony
town. Where's your mother? Will she be home soon?
Sometimes you look like Gene Tierney when you smile—
but you could use some work. If you need money,
check the ceilings. It's where I've hidden the valuables.
They say it's the safest place. No one ever looks
up except maybe that nurse pretending she's talking
to God. She rolls her eyes and recites a few prayers
like that should be enough to convince me she isn't
a Jew-hater. Where's your mother?
She should be home by now.

A Mother's Daughter

Here's to my mother, who gave me
life, who was too young to marry

without her mother's consent, deciding
to elope instead with the man who loved

her, my father, who sent letters home
when he left for the war while she was

pregnant, her belly full with all that I am,
her hair still in pigtails, satin ribbons

the color pink, like the ballet slippers
she once wore before she had to give up

dancing, her days spent alone walking
the garden with her blind dog Blackjack,

conversations I was never meant to hear,
but did, my ears learning her voice, pressed

within the silence of her womb, the nights
she prayed to get through those days alone,

and to be a good mother while she waited
for God to speak to her through nightingales

outside her window—I waited too, though
she never knew how much I would

love her, even then, before I was born. Here's
to my mother, who has long since died, who

I know must be listening from the inside
of a place named Heaven while I'm on

the back porch beneath the lamplight,
speaking to her yet unanswered.

After Admiring a Vintage Portrait in an Antique Store

I'd love to know the unknown histories
of my kin, the legends, myths, and whereabouts
of all who've been before—though old
photographs show stories without words
the more I study them, the more I feel
a traveler back in time, a wanderer

while opening a door that boasts its temporary
sign declaring my existence as fleeting
as a butterfly's with shimmered wings of blue,
the color of my eyes reflected in a mirror, but
who are you? I ask myself as if a voice might
answer—a ghostly echo in my ear.

Years from now, will someone find
my portrait hanging on a wall, nameless
and framed behind some dusty glass, a worthless
heirloom to the passerby, among old memorabilia,
record albums, porcelain dolls that cry,
where antiques and rare collectibles are sold,

one picture of me there forever stilled without
a breath of air? I am the daughter of a daughter
of a daughter, all no longer here. A lineage
of forgotten days—sometimes my mother's voice
rings through the sky like the subtle ping of rain
declaring me a scofflaw when it came to rules

from eras long ago: the sin of drinking alcohol,
playing cards, a game of Gin, a renegade when
my mother's Mormonism was her guiding light.
On my father's side, all European Jews who
prayed on holy days and starlit nights in temples
where the women sat across the aisles wearing

scarves around their pinned-up hair—a way
to segregate, but claimed distraction at its core.
Here's to destiny and fate that blended two
beliefs, creating life from love, my family
tree, the lore they honored son to son
to son, to me, where now I've added pictures

to an album's page, archiving memories
that soon will seem archaic, too. My children
later, glancing through old photos left
behind will sense a plethora of stories
yet untold, secrets saved in snapshots,
faces gazing through eternity's undying

lens morphed with what I've shared
or penned. Is there a time when all we wonder
from our past becomes more clear, when what
we feel of mystery is finally known, or is death
the way we link ourselves eternally to those
who've left us here? Does a photograph

distort our presence once we're gone,
an image appearing very much alive
and vibrant in a moment's flash? Are we
a part of everything or just caught within
two dates that frame the start
and ending of a dash?

Leap Year

When she shares her secrets, you might judge
her for loss of time—staccato memories, recounting
calamity with the hush of a sparrow's last breath,

her lungs emptied of prayers after a stuttering
of darkness, shadows lurking in the corner of her eyes.
Don't worry about the scars on her skin, the long

tear of her body's broken wing, the forever stain
of bruises on the tops of her feet, bones snapped
and butterflied, stapled back together like a robot

in a child's toybox. There are stitches for torn flesh,
titanium plates for jagged bones, but how to give back
the unbrokenness—make her whole again?

And when she wakes at night, her mind powerless
to her body's recall, she will tell you it's nothing.
She will pick feathers from her pillow and try to make

a nest for sleeping, a safe place to cushion
the restlessness of unsaid pain. She isn't quite the same,
her writing a scribble, a nervous twist of cursive,

a quill paralyzed with despair. On a bad night,
her husband will hold her still, *there, there*, he'll say,
and bend her tremors toward the soft hollow

of his core, close her eyes, and whisper a fairy's song
in her ear. She feels safe when he's near. But now
and then the darkness murders her once more,

betrays her sense of calm, and a killing takes place
until she opens her eyes when she's like a book
without a name, a handful of pages ripped

from the middle. That's the problem
with almost dying, it keeps happening
again, and again and again.

Eleven Pipers Piping

On day eleven, since the last day you
said my name, I realized I might never
hear you again. And eleven being a number

of significance, I thought of numerology
and how they term it a "master number"
or a symbol of a Starseed Awakening

which has something to do with synchronicity
in the mystical realm or any realm within the heart's
dominion—and I thought of the way it's

sort of a conniving number or a sum of company,
how it makes two from one, like a double dose
of something with an extra part of another,

and how, in Hebrew, eleven means disorder
which was certainly appropriate for what I
was feeling, and then there's Saint Augustine,

who said eleven is the blazon of sin as if
it was somehow wicked within, or Saint Ursula
who was to be the leader of eleven thousand

virgins later retold as just eleven. So, it could be said
that eleven has been known to exaggerate,
but then nobody wants to say it's the 10th hour

of anything, which is why now, when I think of you
after you'd fallen into a coma, and the eleven days
you never whispered my name or grasped my hand again,

and how it's been eleven years since you've been gone,
and how, in Ireland, the 11th night would be cause for celebration,
we'd be watching fireworks with towering brilliant flames

just before the 12th night, which, as it turns out, was one
night longer than you lived, I think of Shakespeare
and his sonnet 11, and how you must have read

that sonnet, too, holding the words purposely
beneath your tongue while the moonlight
stole your breath away—

she carved thee for her seal and meant
thereby thous shouldst print more, not let that copy die,

as it's only now that I am hearing your message
loud and clear, your voice whispering my name
through the silence, even after all this time, yet

somehow just before the 11th hour.

Aunt Susan

Today, when her cuckoo clock strikes
the hour, it reminds me of being with

her again, back in the garden where
dandelions grew with a hint of yellow

streaming through the air, where she
still waits, lounging in her old plastic

chair, a cigarette in her right hand.
And the clappers dangle and clang

from the golden chain counting hours
with a pause in eternity and the time before

she left. When we'd walk to the river,
our feet wet over the smooth pebbles,

both of us reaching below the coolness
of ripples as we'd hollow the waves for toads,

tipping our glass jars into the water.
We'd watch them swim in, only for us

to free them again, where she taught
me, there is joy in the act of letting go.

Old Painting That Hangs in My House

—Oil on Canvas by Vincente Garcia de Paredes

His rendering of women wearing ballgowns
in shades of irises, men with starched ruffles

at their necks, white petals rising over
skin, the piano more golden than a piece

of jewelry, an angel fingering its keys,
Beethoven filtered through a sunlit room.

I've imagined living in that scene, the parlor
with gleaming bamboo palms, leaves

blooming toward the stained-glass ceiling—
it was my dream as a child to breathe inside

that very image stretched over canvas pulled
taught with tiny staples edged and arched

in the center, allowing enough space
to wedge the tip of a finger beneath metal,

one prong popping out held together
with age, its wooden backing and wire

exposing years of wear. My Grandmother
Hilarita roaming among a roomful

of guests, calling my name with a Spanish
accent. If I could have disappeared into

another life, it would have been there,
instruments filling the chamber, lavender

wafting overhead, gilded still fiddleback
chairs, and me, occupied with everyone,

I'd ever loved, long since dead.

Save Our Souls

When the soldier doesn't come home,
the dog sleeps on his bed,
waits like an abandoned shadow
for a body that will never return.

Weeks later, his wife visits the cemetery—
reads love letters and stares
at a single black crow hovering
above her husband's grassy tomb.

She carefully places a golden letter H
crossways between three dandelions
and a tuft of fallen leaves. They bend
from the weight, the first initial of his name,

as if the universe can't bear the burden
and bows to the heaviness of death—
his life has become an ellipsis she holds
in her hand, like an acronym placed

on a grave. She kneels gently to the carved
headstone, outlining a figure eight with her
middle finger. *This is thievery*, cries the woman
without a husband. *This is thievery,* mocks

the crow with a golden letter H hanging
from his beak. The trees rustle in the wind,
she feels her husband tapping from six
feet under. Morse code; SOS … — — — …

In the Line at Starbucks

I'm in line at Starbucks, waiting for my afternoon
high like all the other 'off to do errands' cars in front
and behind me, and I'm remembering all the lines
I've waited in over the years, and how impatient
and patient I've been depending on what it is I'm waiting for,

and I'm thinking it's so much easier to wait for something
you don't want like the results of an X-ray that portends
bad news, or the yearly mammogram showing some new
visitor in your otherwise contented skin. Whereas the wait
for a cup of coffee sets the afternoon right. That first sip

filling your mouth with a dose of heated joy—and it's the time
of day when the sun looks like a bursting golden flower
hovering in the sky as I spy a cluster of gathered
glory across the road, a field of blooming sunflowers,
soft petals flittering in the wind, bathed in the brilliance—

the sun gushing through a cloud like the God of light.
I'm being patient behind the wheel as I offer up
my order to the guy on the other end of the microphone
who asks about my day and says to move up in line
after I've ordered my latte. But I'm wondering about

the doings of the person in front of me as they too
are following in this quiet single-file line of etiquette.
We are all looking forward to having a hot drink in our hands
before we move on to the next line, wherever that may be—
and just for a minute, we're like those sunflowers huddled

together opening to the warmth—and the attendant smiles
with a potent grin as if he knows he's like the *God of coffee*.
But as I go to pay, he says, "oh, the person ahead of you took
care of your order." To which I say, "thank you," bowing
my head in true sunflower fashion, offering my card

to pay for the person behind me. To which the *God of coffee*
comments, what a gratifying job he has, his grin carrying
me through to another task as I drive off, my fingers
holding onto the unexpected kindness of
someone I will no doubt never meet.

When You're Small, and Your Father Won't Wake Up

Not because she ever thought about
suicide, but because she happened
to be the one who found her parents,
after swallowing handfuls of pills, one

years earlier than the others. And because
her mother remarried when she was still
young, and because that man did the same
after her mother followed in her dead father's

footsteps, so to speak, or at least some invisible
path that led them all to the other side. And for
some reason unknown to her, as if the stars
or fate had a cruel vision that she should be

witness to the lifeless bodies of her parents
after downing clusters of pills, as if they
only saw an aura of light or a chance
at gladness outside their own mortal palms,

as if they heard one answer and never
questioned the swallowing of death, as if there
was something magical about deciding their own
ending and finding courage in requesting God

take you there, a place without the need
or reason to breathe in air, she began
to ponder if they considered who'd find
them, their opened bottles strewn haphazardly

around the floor, hands emptied but for wedding
rings haloing fingers like golden broken promises
before entering eternity. And she began to think
somehow facing that kind of loss made her love

them even more, made her life and theirs extra
precious, made her lament all the years she wouldn't
see them, and she wondered why only one left a note,
which she kept folded beneath her pillow. Only one

said he was sorry. Which made her think he'd
loved her enough to take one moment before
to write it down in faded-blue ink, in shaky script,

on a tiny piece of now yellowed paper. All the words

smeared from a lone tear, as if he didn't want to,
as if he might have reconsidered, as if he'd hoped
someone might have found him
before it was too late.

On the Occasion of Your Mother's Hip Replacement

I tell you, *hips are easy; it's the heart*
that can't be repaired. You say
you'll wait with her overnight—

make her feel at home the way
it used to be when you snored in
the twin bedroom down the hall. I think

how difficult this might be if things
take a wicked turn, if the bleeding doesn't
end, if the need for walking becomes

secondary as hemorrhaging has already
set in. I envision a spare room with handrails
and silver bars, an oversized mechanical

mattress and a full-time nurse giving
orders while sanitizing all things unclean,
even our dog, along with a long list

of new restrictions, as any obstacle
big or small could prove disastrous
for the navigation of someone so frail.

Then I recall my own mother's infirmary
stay, the way they pushed and prodded
and pricked her with needles. How

her arms became black and blue, tattooed
with pin marks like a gathering of indigo stars
on the palest of skin. How she fought back

by yanking out tubes, clutching my hand
and grabbing my fingers as if to beg;
I want to go home, and you're my ticket

out of here. So I say, *let's tell your mother as soon*
as she's well, she'll be staying with us. Just
a little motivation to give her some hope.

We'll paint the ceiling of the spare room with
inspirational quotes. She can't read anymore,
you say. *That's alright; we don't even have a spare room.*

Down by the Watershed

We used to stand face-to-face
across the river, flinging stones
like baseballs in a field. I was young
and you were younger when life
wasn't about anything of real
importance except who could
outfox the other in a game
of truth or dare.

By the end of the day, our mother
would say I was nobody's daughter,
and the very water where I waded
and tiptoed through the middle,
just to be close to you became a place
I'd never want to see again. If only
an angel would have intervened
and saved me from myself after

you'd done your best to wipe me
out with a fistful of sand. My aim,
much better than yours, successfully
blinded your vision for at least
an hour. Something I'm not proud
of yet feel unfairly punished for
even after all these years. Not
that I towered over you, but I had

the advantage of size, though the *whys*,
never seem to matter, especially
when the eyes have it. Meaning
yours was black and blue, and you
certainly took delight in watching me
get the beating of a lifetime, right
there on the beach. Hey, I want
to finally say I'm sorry for that

unfortunate situation, but there
are times I sit back and reflect
on the way you used to egg me on—
still, after all these years, something
tells me if we'd go back in time,
you'd take great joy in tempting fate
again if the same outcome would grant

you another few decades of reveling
in the glory of our mother's sympathy,
even now, long after she's died.

Negotiations Between Things with Plumage

Opening cages one by one, I free
my birds for morning's ritual. They bleat

my name in cockatoo talk, sweet
feathered beings, creatures of hostage.

Today they're perched in the palm
of my hand, the little one pecks the head

of the other. I flick her beak with the tip
of my thumb, she scuttles in rage up

the nape of my neck to the thrum of
obscenities for which I'm sure there are

no translations. I tell her I've seen her kind
before, blameless sufferer that plays

the part, a drama-queen loser without a heart,
the Sarah Bernhardt of beautiful birds,

while the others sit back out of fear
of losing what they believe to be love.

So, I call her out for the sake of honor,
and just as I garner the strength for war,

they fly to their cage. I shut the door,
one crushed quill resting in the hollow

of my hand like a broken spine
of someone I once loved.

After Eating Candy at the Matinee

With his mirror scoping the supple
insides of my jaw, hands, finger
teeth for short fissures and soft
cracks half-broken from wear,

I'm afraid he'll hear the dawdling
leak of evening prayers and leftover
dreams of suicide that seep through
the drool of saliva, my confessions to God.

Here in a dentist's chair, my throat
bared to a man in a white coat
saying open wide, I slide down
a little further in my seat, wondering

if he's noticed the chewed lining of my
inner cheeks and the weariness
of a tongue exhausted from the nightly
grinding of hope, erased by morning's

light. *Bite*, he says, and I stare into
a bright and nameless face. His jacket
dusted with the scent of everyman
and a thimbleful of Novocain for pain.

But I've lost the courage to sit through
his quiet scrutiny. I writhe from side
to side, awaiting a verdict of slow death
by extraction, knowing fate gives then

taketh away. He wheels around the room
and grabs another tool designed for probing
far below the gum line, and I fear before
he's through he'll know all my secrets.

Each one hiding between some deep
crevice in my mouth. I imagine saying
I love you as if his fingers might taste
the words. There's no other way to tolerate

such intimacy from a perfect stranger.

For the Boy Who Swam at Midnight

You are saved in my suitcase of mislaid memories,
hidden away for the time between now and never,
where mysteries are forever stored. Before

I was here or anywhere of importance. A place
to pull you out and lay you away again, the way
a magician hides a rabbit under his hat.

And if you were here, I could make a bad pun
about a hare, and that would make you laugh
because you always said I was funny.

But funny didn't make me prettier
than the cheerleaders whose pictures
lined your wallet, who were waiting half-dressed

outside your dorm room on Friday nights.
Funny was our way into friendship and sharing
parts of ourselves, our bond, an unexpected thrill.

Still, when I heard you pulled a gun to your head
in the middle of the afternoon while blue jays
were singing outside, and magnolias were

in full bloom, I was surprised. I wondered what
you were thinking as you went to your bedroom
and shut the door. Did you kiss your wife one

last time, did you tell her you'd see her on the other
side, did you button your pressed shirt and comb
your hair just the way you always did?

Did you do that quirky smile in the mirror—
turn and say something clever, your nails filed,
your teeth brushed, one last pee, the toilet flushed?

I always imagined I was too full of crazy
in a good way to blend with your idea
of order. But today, memory takes over,

and I allow my heart to follow. To see you
on the floor in all your glory, to scream at you
for not saying you were so troubled, to hold

your wife and let her know it wasn't about her,
to try to remove all the guilt your loved ones
must be feeling. But I only knew you when you

were young, when you saw the world as a small
place you could conquer, when you did laps
in the college pool at midnight, where we'd sneak

in and do one shot of tequila and the whole day
would vanish as I'd watch you swim hour by hour
trying to beat your time, perfecting your stroke,

flicking your blond hair from one side to the next
as little droplets would trail off your golden skin
like tears. Maybe you thought you were your

own God, capable of all things far beyond possible.
Maybe you never considered now and then failure
is okay or just admitting sometimes, life is too hard.

For the Lost Child

There are days she imagines
what it would have been
to have known the child—

the tiniest boy who grew
within her belly, how all
the days that followed

were robbed of promises,
the stories of his life. Poof,
a whole soul vanished

from existence and part of her
as well when his little heart stopped
beating as it pushed one breath

up through her body, past
every tree, when even the birds
stopped singing, and a glorious rain

poured down around her like a mad
tantrum from the sky as if God
were saying, *I want him more.*

Shadows in the Moonlight

—For Larnell Bruce's Mother, whose son was the victim of a hate crime

I wrote a poem for you today,
you whose son was in the headlines,
who died a victim of a hate crime.

I wrote a poem about love,
I wrote a poem about being a mother,
I wrote a poem about death.

But the lines wouldn't come together
though they endured, separate on the page
letters intact, words without meaning—

white against black as they stood
in silence unreadable, each to each
next to the other with nothing to say.

I wrote a poem for you today,
you, whose mother lost her child
who died a victim of a hate crime,

your image fresh in my mind, your eyes
otherworldly and forgiving, even then—
before your death.

And I thought of my own children
and my children's children, and I thought
of the lilacs on the hill and the horses

across the meadow, and warm strawberries
in summer, and the way my son kisses
my cheek, and the nightmare that causes

a scream, and the sound of bullets
from the mouth of anger, and the blood
from the belly that explodes a life,

and the endless verdict of a mother's
suffering in a moonlight filled with abandoned
ghosts, and the way a mother looks at her son,

and the way a son looks at his mother,
and the way a heart can never be unborn.
I wrote a poem for you today.

I wrote a poem about death.

Audrie's Poem

—for Audrie Pott, who died by suicide days after being the victim of rape

You might not know of her, but she
was a mother's answered prayer—given
then taken away. A child with a grown-up body
not yet grown up. They say to be a woman
is to be the giver of life, yet sometimes, without
and even with consent, a body is dishonored,
trespassed, invaded, and a ruining takes place.
Sometimes a monster takes over another,
beats his chest like a wild ogre in a pompous rage,
heaves open her delicate legs, yanks them apart
like a wishbone, her heart pressed empty
leaving a wound vast as a moonless sky.
A thieving of the soul while her eyes were closed,
while she was unconscious, or drunk from the excess
of alcohol, where no one came to save her,
though many stood by and watched, cheered
on the interlopers, her body marked with pens,
a map of all places her intruders had been,
a diagram of sin, a cartography of green lines,
blank was here—blank was here—blank was here—
then left her to find a way back to a place
unreturnable that dug a sorrow so deep
in her breast, breathing became a sadness
that reminded her of something lost, of something
taken, of something shameful, and it was just
so much easier to tie a leather belt around her neck,
let her body smother the darkness out, dangle
from the shower's head with a quick tug of her own
weight as if she could go back to who she was
before the one, two, or three of those monsters raped her—
those heroes to the others who gloated
while her very essence was being murdered
before them, who stayed silent, did nothing
but snap images shared then deleted on phones.
And when their crime was deemed nearly forgivable,
as they walk free, unblemished, unnamed,
will they remember her love of music, of her family,
will they remember her tears, her suicide,
her last text of which she was the giver—
you have no idea what it's like to be a girl.

Minutes from My Doctor's Appointment after My Parents Died.

I told her it was hard to breathe,
and I had a pain level of three—
that somehow, I'd slipped leaving a parked

car. And then I thought about the word
leaving, how a word like that swallows
a life, and how the fallout holds a person hostage.

I miss my parents saying goodnight, tucking
me in and closing my eyes, touching
each lid gently, lashes to lashes,

particles of what once was vanishing in air.
I remember my mother's hairpins
crisscrossed like stars in the dark at bedtime.

When she moved, a glimmer of light
sparked around the room. If only the bars
around my father's bed would've kept him safe,

he might not have wandered so far. He was
always searching for someone as if he'd
misplaced himself.

He was formidable, even without his teeth.
He'd spit pomegranate seeds into a glass
jar like chewed-up hearts,

one after another. Once, he sauntered
through the doorway of a lady's house
and asked to stay over. When I picked

him up, he said his mother would be worried.
I've always felt lost in the memories of someone
else, of bathing my mother in lavender oil,

of reading my father's favorite prayers, of cleaning
out their drawers, of having them to worry about.
And when that nurse took my vitals, I wanted

to say, no! I wanted to take them back.
I never thought it was easy to get old,
but there's something sinister about watching

age take over. Hands wither up, legs get weak, and I could see death hiding, right there in the room with me.

Cigars, Cigarettes, and Me

He's the cabby who plays to a Brazilian
beat in wanderlust syncopated rhythm,

and I imagine an unborn child slumbering
somewhere deep inside; if only our ride

began a few years back when the girl
from Ipanema was blowing her horn.

My shoulders samba then glide in this vehicle
hailed by me where I see traffic lights

bleed through city rain on a cold day
in San Francisco. He turns and says,

*you have the bluest eyes. Do you know
the Bossa Nova? Yes, I'm a real Bim Bom*

Freak. Two lies, but the Orpheum's straight
ahead. I wish I smoked at a time like this.

I tell him the Copacabana is grander
than any bar I've ever seen. My dress is black

and green with a mean décolletage, and I lean
in to check the fare, my breasts overflowing

like river pears, and he beams in exaltation.

The Boyfriend?

I'm the guy who looks prettier than you,
who wears Zegna suits and cufflinks
with my initials in gold.

I've been told I'm great in bed, and that's
an understatement unless you underline
great in red, then you'd be on the mark.

Here's my card, it's white, stark
except for the bold letters spelling
my name. I'm the same asshole you

dated in school who was too cool
to call you back, ask you out for a second
date, never showed up, or brought you

home defiantly late, your dad at the door
pacing beneath the lamplight. He knew my
type with my lopsided grin and arrogant

chin. Listen, I'm the one-night stand
every girl needs to shatter their Pollyanna
heart. I'm a master at the art of being

a dick. I'm a real prick with a diamond ring
under my tongue. I'm like a ventriloquist
with a thousand quips. I can breathe the words

I Love You from your very own lips.

In Another Life

In another life, I held a woman
in my arms and licked her lips
tinged with honey. I wore a veil

and thin black ribbon with a cameo
resting at the delicate curve
of my throat—the place where skin

hollows to the shape of bone,
and one finger's press can stop
a breath in motion.

In another life, I turned her hair
between my hands and braided
violets for the petticoat she hid

beneath her velvet skirt.
I loved her on a bed of grass
under the noonday sun—

there's a hint of madness
in a love like that, a love that
shouldn't be—

like the key that hung from
a long chain above my mother's
jewelry case taunting me

all those years. Exhilarating to imagine
the trinkets inside—I knew
they would be beautiful

yet unthinkable to touch and remain
in the realm of being a good girl.
In another life, I would

have defied the rules, stretched further
than my own reach, beyond the place
of obeying correctness.

I would have unlocked that box,
revered the gems, frolicked
in the inaccessible, save the guilt

like an unfettered prisoner in all her glory.

Homage to this Heart

This heart is half wing, half song,
part of each child carried from my
womb through daylong

gatherings of gardenias.
This heart is fuller when it doesn't
need to be—

when no one's counting on it.
It plays hide and seek with its owner—
and doesn't cry in public but weeps

on a pillow during nighttime hours,
it holds secrets of belladonna remedies
to anyone who can't be kind—it's like

a miniaturist's piece of art but essential
to the rest of me, even when it wills
itself to a piqued state. It thrives

on a lexicon of love, twists in and out
of madness. It's a scar-filled, amputated
bionic thing with a bright flare inside,

and not even the cruelest death
in spring can stop its craving for light.

Tiny Mercies

Grandmother, you were a chrysanthemum
lover, a grower of dahlias and wild peaches
in the garden. Your house surrounded

with bindweed vines, sweet peas,
and long-stem chaparral clematis.
This is my love letter to you, my homage

to your hidden scars while your throng
of blossoms grew as you tended your garden,
hummingbirds in your hair. Celadon gloves

over arthritic fingers, I watched you comb
the earth, dress it with blooms until
your hands became part of the soil,

digging through and making way for roots
to grab on beyond the winter wren's last song
of summer. After the death of a husband,

two sons, one then the other, living through
both world wars and the Great Depression,
your garden never looked unkempt.

Tiny buds sprouted periwinkle blue
as stems pressed against the white weather
worn arbor. Did they cry to you in evenings

when your heart lay awake? Did your mornings
break to the silent opening of flowers before
you'd serve me cereal for breakfast, peaches

quartered, soft half-moons baked in sugar?
Am I doing enough? Does it matter
with all the dysfunction in the world? I stay up

evenings counting stories, chronicles of the days
bad news. I dream of a place I can't name
anymore, faded like the sepia photographs

of everyone I've loved who's passed.
This is my message to you, my hushed tantrum
with no reply. Won't you send me a canticle

of answers, an obsequious nightingale
from your old garden? I have grown chrysanthemums
in your honor, tended dahlias and sweet peas

on even my worst days. Tiny mercies thriving,
their colors drape the air in healing shades of lavender.
They don't care about the problems of the universe.

They're happy with what I give them, unconcerned
about their fate. They're my passage between today
and tomorrow, my body weighted to the ground,

my knees pressed in prayer-like pause, my hands
holding your rose-water tool, while I remember
you, asleep in your flora-covered coffin.

Terms of Endearment and a Grandmother's Word

Pyracantha berries grew near my grandparents'
garden and smelled like my grandmother
in winter after the years swallowed her joy—
the death of her son to suicide.

She tried to be happy on days
I'd stay with her, my mother off doing
whatever mothers do when a husband has died,
still putting food on the table the best she was able.

My grandmother's house, littered with old
photos of long-ago pictures from before
I was born as though she was torn between
an illusion of yesterday's truth and all that followed.

She called me *Liebchen* when I was small.
A name that sounded sweet even
without a German accent, yet cloaked
with a tinge of sorrow, the way a word can't help

its delivery when said aloud. I knew she
was eager to die. She held a permanent
view of mourning in the corner of her eye.
Her knitting needles crisscrossed then stilled,

hands paralyzed and wrapped around the next
pearl of yarn, a death prayer floating between
old memories and time. A crime of grief right before
me, though I was too young to understand that kind

of loss. I watched those berries bloom every year
with robust desire, red flames on fire, hungry robins
niggling at them through the window of her lanai.
Little alcoholics, she called them. *Liebchen*

she'd say as if a sugar tear had just rolled off
her tongue—*those birds are getting drunk
on my berries*, and we'd laugh at the sight,
watching them wobble away in a sluggish flight.

All those years, we never spoke of my father's
suicide. His story buried six feet under with a stomach
full of pills as if it wasn't true—a family secret
we were too ashamed to share.

But I was there, the one who found him, though
unaware he'd left a note on the table, tucked inside
a white leather-bound Bible saved in my mother's
nightstand drawer. *Liebchen* means dear, even

when there's no one left to call you over, to sit beside
them and watch the birds. Turns out those berries
never made those birds tipsy. They were just gluttonous
little beggars too full to fly, poor naïve things.

It's easy to know the makings of a lie if part
of it becomes your story, too. Pretty soon,
no one knows the difference,
even you.

Regarding Your Submission

Though we appreciate the effort
you took, we're very sorry
for the postage stamps you've wasted
in your attempt to deliver poetry.

We did enjoy a few lines
that showed promise, especially
the one comparing death
to an embryonic state of being.

But it wasn't enough to move
us or send a shiver down Mary's
telekinetic spine, and we're convinced
she is the barometer for all promising

poems; not that we need a mind reader
to set the bar for our decisions,
but paranormal abilities transcend
the norm, and so we call this the Mary Test—

which, unfortunately, you did not pass.
My best advice would be to read,
read, read. Unlock something new
from a warbled dream, a disturbing

experience. Find the grandeur
in what seems absurd. Consider
the life of an ant, for example.
I've used a magnifying lens once

or twice to angle the sun's rays
enough to scorch an insect or two
in hopes of writing a masterful poem.
I assumed the incident would lend itself

to something metaphorically pleasing
as I watched them fight for their tiny
lives. Regrettably, Mary shared
with me later that my poem

came by way of cruelty, therefore
it was discounted greatly
when reviewing my work.

The trick is to confuse the audience

to the point where they have no idea
what you're talking about, and if your
poems come on Friday, there's a good
chance we'll have had a couple

of shots of tequila, which makes
for more positive responses
since Mary usually eats the worm.

To the Editor Who Knew Me from My Poems

I hear you through the words,
a stirring in leaves, your punctuation
marking poems—

lines of red crossing out errors,
your hand a weapon of strokes.
Where is your last page now—

your final critique guiding me
through the process
as if there was no life beyond poetry,

beyond the binding of numbered pages.
In your letters, illness pervaded, a course
of remedies pending each wearying stage.

I began to fear your death in the middle
of knowing the ending even before
there was a way to mark the center,

your unplanned farewell. There was always
a prelude of hope, until there wasn't—
each new treatment your body suffered

the failures of being human, weakness
filling your veins until the day your blood
bled clear. There is no beauty

in dying, no way to erase this for that.
When your wife wrote to me,
I wanted to soothe her, to say you'd made

a difference. Forgive me; I did not know
her loss, yet you are still alive
in my writing, your absence a gaping dash

within. You, who spoke of palmettos
in summer, your fondness for mountains,
and the way your legs could no longer travel—

a desk became your life, your portal
to the world. Your messages
more brief as fingers lost their will.

I never said thank you before you died,
before you knelt on the cold night floor,
hunched over your beloved books

the way I've imagined—as they held you
up, became a part of you until you could
recite them all from memory, even mine.

Cat Remembers Being Young

—for Suki, my Siamese cat, my first love

I'm lost to dreams of what life once was
when we lived in that old house, the one
where this story began, the house I'd hoped
to live in forever, yet nothing lasts forever,
even my dreams are broken before ending.
But I like lingering on the before rather than after.
Her little bed, with its gold-sprayed headboard,
and handmade quilt she pulled over us
while napping. Her window, where I viewed
the world beyond, and the stillness that surrounded
the hours, where stephanotis brushed against
glass, a flurried reminder of wind marking time.

It was a place of sun-drenched afternoons,
of cruising old neighborhoods in her painted
red wagon as it rolled along the walkway rimmed
with tiny block houses in green, pink, and yellow,
my tail unfurling in all directions as it sliced
through the blueness of air. The overgrown
willow with its elongated leaves that drooped
in handfuls of sallow green down the driveway,
tiny bits of itself cluttering our path to the front yard.
Petunias bursting over the splintered edge
of the planter box in too many colors to count.
There was more of everything back then,
and she was still there, my paws kneading
the heart beneath her chest as she cradled
my body and stroked my fur.

Oh, to the days of catching an ill-fated
mouse, bringing it back to the steps of that house,
to her, the one who loved me, who kept me
close yet gave me the freedom to roam
from tree to tree in search of sparrows,
magpies or squirrels running free. Our
afternoons filled with wonder, ending
with a warm bowl of milk, eight lives still
to follow, since lost to years and fate,
as she abandoned me for something
called college. Now I laze across the sunlit
grass and consider how my purring has become

complacent, hollow as if a concession for having
to go on without her.

Perhaps this is acceptance, or maybe
death quietly birthing from within as the heart
begins to acquiesce and change in its silent shift
that's always paired with grief. Her mother
ousting me to ominous oaks on the hillside,
forcing me to grapple with the wilderness of nature
after breaking her beloved Chinese lamp,
one she never used yet placed thoughtlessly
on the edge of a marble table, with its long cord
catching my paw in an unfortunate accident
without the girl to defend me.

Though, I have no shame in breaking
her mother's things. Stupid collectibles that cluttered
my route from room to room, hindering my path
in what seemed a deliberate array of breakables.
Today, I tap my tail against a dandelion while
admiring my ageless shadow as it looms in
distorted angles beneath the afternoon heat.
I stare and meow at leaves the color of sage
as I navigate the badlands and ponder memories
of the good old days, yet with a sense of indifference.
Just now, a rattlesnake is creeping toward me.
It serpentines across the lawn and slithers near.
I hear its sibilant sound never once
having the urge to hiss.

Listen, Darling

I know that memory has haunted you
for years. The day you were shopping
with your grandmother. She was such a proper
lady, and there you were, standing beside
her as she tried on clothes in front

of a three-way mirror. You can still
hear the lilt in her voice when she said
said, *come here, darling,* smoke
billowing from her mouth as it wafted
over fingers dressed in diamonds,

the scent of cigarettes filling the air.
Your hair wound in a bun, a strand of flowers
pinned behind your ear, your uniform
pressed, a little gold brooch on your
pinafore. It was *The House of Quan Yin.*

Her favorite store. And she was so busy trying
on clothes, her arms full of silks in every shade
of blue. Maybe it was because you could've
said something but instead pretended not
to see when that woman strolled out wearing

a stolen coat. She glanced over with a short
loving kind of stare, and it was like having a secret
with a stranger. Some part of you liked the intimacy
of that exchange, like you were an accomplice,
or maybe saving her, and she knew.

Your grandmother just kept shopping, stopping
for puffs of her cigarette as if she was in another
world long enough for you to share in a moment
that's never left. And that coat had a good life,
hanging in that woman's closet for decades.

She took such care of it, bringing it out between
seasons, checking for moths, brushing the collar
to keep the luster of its fur. She wore it to her daughter's
wedding, her husband's funeral, and then
she was buried in it, the price tag still folded

in the left pocket. Every time you've put on
a coat since you've felt grateful you didn't have
to steal it—but part of you has always wondered
if your grandmother knew all along—taking a slow
drag off her Pall Mall, flicking ashes from her ring,

quietly whispering, *just add it to my bill.* Like that woman's
coat was part of her haul for the day. Because you
remember her compassion, and sometimes
if you close your eyes, you can almost hear her
say, *don't worry darling, I took care of it.*

Dear Penny's Lingerie Police

I'm writing to let you know that in 7th grade,
I stole a 34 triple-A bra. It feels cathartic to admit
to a moment of thievery that's haunted me all these years.
But having a mother who cherished innocence more
than my growing up made puberty a crime of its own,
along with the want for girly unmentionables.

You might even say I was pushed to stealing
the afternoon our neighbor sat across from me
at our kitchen table, eating a bowl of ice cream,
when I felt a chill, and he said, *Hey, your nickname
could be Pop-Art*. A movement I found made famous
with a painting titled *Drowning Girl* by Roy Liechtenstein,

where she's giving in to the ocean's current with
a thought bubble placed over her head that read,
"I'd rather sink than call Brad for help!" My nipples
must have been poking through my top like two
sprouting buds from the rosebush outside. Later
that day, I rode the bus to the mall and meandered
over to lingerie, probing aisles for lacy things,

avoiding the lady guarding the dressing room with her
long yellow measuring tape draped around her neck,
formidable as a doctor's stethoscope. That bra left
the store beneath my pinafore, and I might have been
guiltfree all these years, but for my neighbor's crudeness,
and my mother's prude(ness), and all that surrounds
the melodrama of being 13. Still, it feels good
to finally get this off my chest.

Sincerely, *Who's Brad?*

The Day I was a Visiting 2nd Grade Teacher

Today, I'm reading *Stellaluna* to a room of seven-year-olds—
a story about a bat in a world of birds. They're watching
me with great interest, and I feel like I'm a youngster again,
wanting them to like me. I'm remembering days

of being in line for hot soup at the Convent, raising
my hand to be called on, and the way we sat in perfect
rows at awkward righthanded desks, me being lefthanded.
It's easy, I think, to pull this off, to have them like me.

I smile as I read and emphasize the funny parts
of the story. The words the author uses, the onomatopoeia,
the oofs, and eeks surrounding the failing flights
of newly flying things in the dark. There's a certain

amount of potty mouth going on in the background.
A distraction that fills the room with on-and-off laughter,
the tallest boy making what he calls poop noises,
mimicking a bird squatting on the ground. I laugh

and pretend it doesn't bother me as the jokes whirl
about in near silence, regurgitated by the girls
sitting in the front row. I, too, am distracted by gestures
that seem to imply the inappropriate, yet I read on.

It's amusing to me to feel the humor and the frustration
of being mocked and observed at the same time.
When the story is finished, I thank the class for listening,
and we all clap as I pick up my things to leave.

One boy, the one who created the ruckus at
the start, scurries over and throws his head
in my stomach, his arms wrapped closely around
my body, his whole self leaning in. I put my hand

on the back of his head, caressing his soft hair
as he brushes against me. *Thank you*, he says,
looking up at me, his eyes full of mischief and joy—
and for that moment, I want to be his mother,

kiss his cheek and say he's forgiven for the undercurrent
of chaos he brought that day. So, I make a poop noise,
and we both laugh, and I feel grateful for a moment
of silliness that gave us a connection without words.

The Haunting

Someone once asked if all my poems were about my mother.
Yes, I said as if there was a way to write without her
showing up, as guilt, as love, as tenderness or even
the shadow of her image in the mirror. That's her now, standing

there, behind the door, that sliver of light seeping in this room.
I wanted to say she follows me everywhere, no matter
where I am or where I've been. In the hometown
where I grew up, I left a backyard full of buried pets

and a litany of prayers veiled with overgrown grass, a resting
place for birds, turtles, and beloved dogs, popsicle stick
headstones marking all their graves, tiny crosses saved
from a childhood long ago. I wonder if the people who live there

now have removed them. I mean, it's not like you can
take death with you. It doesn't travel well; it waits where
it once lived and remains forever at its final destination
as if it's saying time does stop, long enough to remove

this piece of you. Then, it begins again, with a kind
of indifference nearly unbearable in its unpredictability.
But if you are lucky, now and then, part of death slips
through a door or just an opening in a broken

sky like a trespasser in the night searching for its past,
only its past is you or some part of you. At my mother's
funeral, my children stood beside me, and the pastor
read the eulogy I'd written. I wanted to read it myself,

but he thought I'd never get through it. Today, I'd like
to tell him I didn't get through it. I'm still there, in that
chapel, waiting to read what I wrote, and so it comes
out in all my poems as if my mother might be carefully

listening, or maybe annoyed, I wasn't strong enough
to let time stop and take her, and so she continues
to survive the part of her that was removed, the part
that doesn't know she's dead. In our new house

I haven't buried one pet in the yard, but when
I open the freezer and see a box of popsicles,
I can't eat them; I'm saving them out of fear,
out of spite, out of grief, a way of freezing time

as if I could go back and explain to that pastor
that my mother is still waiting for me to recite
those words I wrote for her so many years ago,
so she can finally hear what I have never been

willing to say out loud—*goodbye.*

Excavation of an Expired Womb

No one wants to tell you, your body
will betray you, especially when you're
young, before the takedown, not even
the ones who've gone before.

They are the secret keepers. Mother
from daughter, sister from sister, friend
from friend. This slow change within,
an unhurried pace, a silent adagio

of slowed tempo speed until the time
your body fails you. Your insides
caving in, pushing their way through
like creeping lilacs in search of the sun

as if they're trying to escape, see past
an opening, tiptoeing around to the outside.
And one day, you'll wonder when you're in
the doctor's office, his hands prying

you apart like a wishbone, why no one warned
you. How your own shadow of softness
turned against itself? How an age war took
over in a hushed revolt like a silent coup

when all the while, every older woman you knew
stood by and watched you ogle at yourself,
thinking your body unstoppable, knowing
you'd have an expiration date, like a cold jug

of milk, a dozen delicate eggs or hand-sliced
meat from the butcher. And that doctor will slide
his chair back and forth, back and forth,
sucking on a piece of hard rock candy, his teeth

clicking and cracking on edible sweets
as he delivers surprising news. He'll schedule
your stay between a moment of panic, your willing
submission, when he'll mine your heart,

cut out your sacred parts where the tiniest
flowers once grew in mauves and lavenders,
sweet baby hues. And you'll get through
it somehow, never speaking about it,

your tender tongue weighted with saved
stories untold, your eyes fixed in an almost
cataleptic state. And when you're alone,
you'll remember your loveliness, savoring

memories of your youth as you lounge
on your bed, exhausted from the journey.
But something will be missing, some hallowed
piece of your soul, and a toll will have

been taken to get you from there to here—
as if you'd been hunted from afar like the nine
tailed fox from The Sunrise Valley, and when
you look in the mirror, you won't know who you are.

Song Dynasty

—In 19th century China, when women were footbound

When my feet are bound, they'll make
a lovely pair of lilies, and my husband
will celebrate the hollow beneath
my anklebone. When my pain oozes
blood, my skin will weep, and I will fill
the stream with tears beneath my window
as I gaze at the cherry tree dropping
petals like eyelashes through wind.

I will know there's good reason for this,
my four toes bent backward, folded
onto themselves, each foot growing
into a golden lotus tangled in the roots
of my bones—until one day, they break
from bindings, from being without
air, and walking on my own skeleton.
My arch aching, broken and regrown,

silk tied and retied around my skin,
my feet the size of a thumb or a man's
genitals. How beautiful I'll be as I take
my miniature steps back and forth
across the dirt floor packed so tight,
wet from my tears. I will cry to my mother
and my mother's mother, and beg
for escape from tradition. No, they

will say this will make you marriageable,
this will make your pelvis strong; this
will ensure your womb is indeed bountiful,
this will make you unable to run through fields
and dance in the meadows. This will be
a ritual of honor, a declaration of wealth
though some may die of infection,
of a murdered heart, of teeth piercing

the dark night with screams. Loss is always
inevitable, and this is our custom passed
down through generations. This is the yin
and yang of life. This will make you
subordinate to men; this will make you
a good wife.

How to Fall in Love with Robert Bly

Rest a book of his on the kitchen table next
to your coffee cup topped with cream.
Turn on morning music and swallow

his words with each sip of breakfast blend.
Raise the curtains and watch the golden
finches fly back and forth between long vines

in search of berries. Rest a book of his
on the kitchen table, and open it with
the gentle grace of touching a child's face.

Remember, there is company in solitude,
and sometimes, it's the loneness that fills
the space. Rest a book of his on the kitchen

table, and think of the cows drinking rainwater
across the meadow, and the sheep grazing
on high grass near the river, their bodies

warm as a mother's breast. Cry for the world's
willingness to ignore the unknown, know that your
weeping is heard by a sky teeming with stars.

Rest a book of his on the kitchen table,
and open it sweetly like the midnight
turndown of a coverlet on a forgiving bed—

exhaust yourself with memories of the dead
until your whole being is a living ghost
of all the people you've lost, your arms

weak from holding grief and a thousand
letters written on clouds through a stream
of sunlight thin as a strand of hair—

tell your children you will always be there,
that you'll never leave, though leaving is certain
as suicide in silence, inevitable as men

turning away from love. Rest a book
of his on the kitchen table, and imagine
him reading *The Untempered Soul*.

Put your hand on the pages and touch
the drums. Run your fingers through
unseen air in figure eights. Lookup

existence in the dictionary—it will say
something that exists. Lookup
nonexistence in the dictionary—it will

be there despite its absence.
Rest a book of his on the kitchen table
because no one knows what it does between

readings on days you've looked away,
abandoned your own heart in search
of another's—his book will be waiting

for the white windowed light, opened,
and unopened, read, and unread,
whether you know it or not, until his poems

are a part of you, have found their way home,
where they'll live and breathe, leave and enter
just as the golden finch carries on,

comes and goes in spite of your absence.

Handful of Stallions at Twilight

>   *—For my father,* Army Corporal, 7 Ordnance, Korea
>   Golden Gate National Cemetery Plot: 2C 4599

Thoughts on what's left behind—

The memory of a houseful of mourners,
my aunt as she opened the old Frigidaire, saying,

*Be strong for your mother—here
are your dinners for the next hundred days.*

Our old dog, Blackjack, who slept
on your favorite pillow. The two years

he napped there as if you'd come home
then died in the loneliness of waiting.

I still remember the hollow of your eyes,
how shadows lurked through a haze of brown.

What voice must have said, *there's no more
happiness, surrender, take this handful of pills.*

They say heroes die in battle. Do some
face the enemy once they've come home?

And where are your medals, your ribbons
of honor for winning a war?

Here, this souvenir, this gathering
of stars, this American flag that covered

your casket while buglers played the day
you were buried to the sound of Taps.

I've saved your drawings, your pictures
of stallions, and notes that you scribbled,

your jumbling of thoughts. Did you write
the answers on the bark of a tree?

Will it one day rot, too weak to stand, fall
onto itself against the cold earth, its canopy

of leaves splayed over ground, your sadness
removed where a cluster of dandelions rise

wild and free? Who will know the sorrow
that came to you? Or was it joy—

a vision of angels carved from stone,
a golden gargoyle adorned at the gate?

When I found you, your cheek still kissable,
your skin the shade of water and sleep,

but too much time had passed to save you.
What life is so eclipsed by grief

death becomes a wanted thing? Was your last
goodnight an escape or apology?

Did you see an opening through a pinhole
in the sky, a path beyond darkness to moonlight?

Maybe you hoped someday I'd follow?
Was death so sweet a promise no daughter

could call you back? In my dreams, your horse
gallops on the meadow; the one you drew

from a black and white sketch. Sometimes
you're the rider; sometimes, there's just a horse.

Rage at My Father's Illness

Let's try to remember the way from here
to there. I'll go over it once more, and you
be sure to make mental notes along the way.

Mark the road inside your head with short,
invisible lines between all signs pointing
beyond a mental labyrinth every day. You're

the bead, weighted, dropping through a hole.
If I were nicer, I wouldn't be thinking about
tomorrow while trying to get us through today.

I wouldn't say things like, remember when?
Since you've already forgotten the details
taking great delight in reinventing history

in your new aloof, unfatherly style. I'll file
you under once upon a nightmare, knowing
this isn't easy on either of us. You barely

notice the difference anymore while I'm forced
to struggle with your continual insistence
of never being wrong. There are days I hate

you for that, and for not knowing when I hate
you, or how impatient I've become, or how
unkind I've been. Yet I love you for knowing

I love you, even when you've lost yourself
to memories and doubt in this comatose
mode of being within and being without.

When an Interruption in Your Contentment Takes Place

That dream, that hideous dream, where someone's baby,
not yours, leans over the crib, and you're too far away
to catch him as he tumbles forward—and you pause
in horror, watch it happen, his head hard against the marble
floor, both of you caught in that space between slumber
and awake, where the nightmare holds you hostage,
your body numbed by sleep, your heart a separate
entity, as you witness the catastrophic and the world
going on without you. Your guilt, as if you could
have saved it.

When you're getting dressed, that memory of your mother,
your dead mother as she sits on a chair in your closet
while you try on clothes and nothing looks good,
and she tells you so, shakes her head, giving her opinion—
the red dress too tight, the sweater too low-cut,
the skirt pencil-thin, emphasizing the shape of your butt
when you turn sideways, splitting when you bend over,
the zipper's teeth cockeyed from the trauma, but you pin
it together, wear it anyway, walk away in defiance,
a long cardigan over your arm.

That afternoon, that long afternoon when you were at the vet's
office, when the receptionist asked you about your day while you
were waiting for the doctor to look at your dog, who wasn't feeling
well, who'd kept you up all night with her nausea, ruining
your comforter and everything else she came in contact with—
and when they called your name, you smelled an awful thing,
so you looked down to see if vomit was decorating your jeans,
relieved nothing was there until you looked over your shoulder
and noticed a big shit on the chair where you'd been
sitting. One giant poop from your dog who thought nothing
about it, who wagged her tail and licked your face as you wiped
it up, and you were just grateful it wasn't a messy one.

That evening, that embarrassing evening when
the nurse who took care of your senile dad suffering
from bad dementia; your dad, who you'd found hitchhiking
earlier that week, who liked to wear a CIA t-shirt
to the neighborhood church, swearing he was an
intelligence operative, called to say she was quitting.
Tired of his advances, the last straw after being
humiliated at the local pharmacy while picking

up prescriptions, when he winked and asked
the clerk for a box of condoms, the x-large size,
he added, and there was nothing she could do
but buy them, as he smiled and grabbed her hand.

That text, that awkward text you sent to your friend
when you were excited about the poetry event, telling
her the details. You, going on and on about this and that
and the two new boobs you were bringing to the event.
Books! The two new books you were bringing! *Lol,*
she wrote in her text back. And then that picture you
included, asking for her opinion—too tomboy, ugly,
not ugly? I've seen you look better, she said.
THE SHIRT you texted back in capital letters.
I was only asking about the shirt!

Memo to My Children

They are different now. They are daylight
after the evening moon falls out of my hand
and rolls beyond the stars. I'm not able

to keep them and kiss their cheek or unravel
a dandelion in their palm where a wish
used to live windborne and unbranched.

But I say to them, I am still your mother.
I am the bone that breaks when you tumble
from a hollowed tree. I am the sorrow

of all prayers that hover unheard. I am
the reflection in a raindrop that lands
on your windowsill tomorrow, tomorrow, and tomorrow.

It will always be this way, though you may
never understand the home that was lost
when you grew up and found your place

in the world. The home that sits up at night
and counts little teeth in a miniature mug saved
under the bathroom sink where the tooth

fairy kept everything, even your pillowcase
with scribbled marker—your names
in five-year-old scrawl across the soft, pale fabric.

Oh, children, tell me how to forget the scent
of tangerine in your hair, your face pressed
against my breast after a bad dream—

your chair where I rocked you to sleep
to your favorite lullaby played on the old music
box still here on my bedside table—know you will

always be mine as you walk through every
morning. I am there, tethered to your shadow,
the rumble in your heart though you run free.

Epistolary Thoughts from an Aging Schoolgirl

They thought I knew you'd died, so I lied
and pretended I'd heard that, too.
And when I stood in the courtyard

where we used to hopscotch
with long lines of chalk nearly visible
in concrete squares from yesteryears,

I thought how ironic that I'd be there
without you. All those promises
from fingers pricked to bleeding,

pressed together like a steeple's door.
But you always had that faraway look
in your eye, as if something crazy

was looming within, as if you'd choose
a wild ride over well-being, and I just knew
when they said you'd passed, it was better

not to ask because I'd always thought
I'd see you again, and knowing the truth
would've broken me in ways I can't explain.

The Gingham Dress

The girl in the picture who wore that gingham
dress looked so omniscient standing there,
her long legs crossed, one foot tipped, resting

on a bottom stair, untangled hair. She appeared
unworried in that dress, and I wondered if she'd read
the paper that day or ever heard bad news—

the way she stood; her left shoulder dropped
low against the backdrop of a pink-painted wall,
her buttons undone, she seemed blasé,

indifferent to it all. She was tall, her stare
a half dare like a warrior draped in cotton woven cloth.
One hand slipped inside a pocket as if a secret

weapon was beneath her checkered print.
Did she watch the morning market rise and fall?
Did she even care while wearing that gingham

dress, or was it like a flag of freedom from
what ails you? No running broadcast could rock
a girl like that who smiled without a blink,

no *Breaking News* of a shooter's spree or victim's
broken cry from bullets fired across a parking lot.
No, that girl could watch an airplane crash,

the shrapnel gash her cheek, spit, and slick
a rebel curl behind her ear. She could pepper
spray a grocery clerk to steal a loaf of bread

then eat it on the way to buying one more dress—
or perhaps she'd helped the poor then gave
the homeless hope with flowery prayers,

and donated her kidney without a care,
or volunteered for twenty good deeds a day.
I liked the way the fabric folded into accordion

pleats against her hips, her hand turned upwards,
full of hope, a resting spot for lost birds, her fingertips
extending toward the stars. *La Vie*

was written in calligraphy across the page
as if that dress could change a life. But it was
that girl I wanted to know—and ask her if

she wore it every day? If it helped her look
so stoic, the way she almost gloated with her lips
apart. A fearless dame, as if she'd saved a life,

 or maybe ate her lover's heart.

When Last That Sadness Bloomed

When we moved from the old house,
I was tired of the memories even before
we'd left. Exhausted from the mourning

that filled doorways past the blue blur
of agapanthus where once I stood holding
my mother's hand, when she smiled

and told me to plant lavender roses in the garden—
which I did, yet had to leave behind when they
were in bloom, midsummer, after a long winter

of being dormant. Where my mother-in-law's
voice became an everyday cry over the receiver,
an alarm system sounding each time

we'd say goodbye. Where now, after she's gone,
that phone has stopped its ringing. I hear
its silence as I gaze out the front window

at the stephanotis lining our walkway endwise,
reminding me of being little again and my childhood
home where they grew, where there was no

alarm system, only my father, who paced
the entry and examined the porch in the gloaming
twilight for footprints and cigarette butts. His ritual

sacred as evensong, certain someone was there
hiding beneath the willow tree. He never lived long
enough to grow tired of that house. I wonder

now, which home will be my last? Who will be
left to pack up my collectibles, to reminisce
and lament old stories and all the history

surrounding them, forced to leave something
beyond memories behind, a lavender rose,
a father, a mother, me?

The Benediction

Prayers for daffodils as they moon their way
in radiant yellows, pristine petals trumpeting
grace, warmed by the sun, among all creatures
wild and small, where we are one,
where we are all—

Praise every saintly thing on earth.

Prayers for wild grasslands rising near
Heavens through temporary space, moving soft
clouds, their shrouds in easy dawning light
where every wish from me to you
comes true—

Praise every saintly thing on earth.

Prayers for each heart within a constellation's
ring—I'll write a song for you today and sing
it 'til it vibrates goodness everywhere
knowing God is here, knowing God
is there—

Praise every saintly thing on earth.

Prayers for harmony and a choir of angels;
intimate as hands that brush an eyelash
from a face or dreams where secret gardens
dance, and everyone is blessed beyond
infinity retraced—

Praise every saintly thing on earth.

Prayers for faith and harmony, divine
completeness, the rivers, lakes, the sea,
and even me, ramshackle, broken body,
with hope for all life and a better destiny—

Praise every saintly thing on earth.

Prayers for beauty as it blooms over
valleys and hills where flowers unfurl,
ours to share, where love might flourish
in the tiniest breath and thrive in every
child while we're alive—

Praise every saintly thing on earth.

Prayers for a Star that marks our place
of birth, where highlands are full of blossoms
and evening bells that chime, where our spirits
will rise above each wrong to do what's right,
where you'll put your hand in mine—

Praise every saintly thing on earth!

Empty Nester

How do you ask your sons to come home
when they no longer need you to rock

them to sleep? Come home to a place
that doesn't exist; their rooms

long abandoned of childish things.
Yet you are their mother, the maker

of princes, your castle now emptied
of gold swords and crowns. Will they be

nobler than what you'd imagined, will they
slay monsters and three-legged beasts,

and name you in speeches with fairytale endings
for all that you taught them or all that you didn't?

While You Were Having Your Colonoscopy

While you were having your colonoscopy—
I remembered my dad and his last appointment
for the same test, who, before they called his name,

ate a glazed donut in the waiting room
as if he planned an interruption of the process,
making sure there'd be no procedure

that day. One donut putting a halt to everything—
one donut between findings and no findings,
between growth or no growth. One donut keeping

him from knowing his fate. But you are not
a donut taker. There will never be one donut
between you and anything. So, while you were

having your colonoscopy, I was pacing
the waiting room, searching the countertops
for glazed donuts or something a little bit sweet

as if that could pause the outcome—a silly notion
since you were the one having a test, which
is why I was thinking of my dad in the first place,

and how brave you are, how you never grab
the donut, even if it's right there within reach,
and how I try my best to be like you on most

days, even though, like my dad,
I have a strong proclivity for donuts.

Forgive Me

I was never meant to be your Jesus,
though my hands were open, palms upturned to sky—
this might have fooled the vulnerable who begged
for more than those around could give.

Should I have warned you when you asked for prayers
and bread? Sometimes, the demons played inside
my head. Although, from outside in, appearances
portrayed the softest freesia-face

allowing certain mayhem—still, a trace
of crumbs was left behind for you. One tiny trail
you'd take requesting your deliverance. But oh, that walk
was blinded with indifference, some leafy camouflage,

as if umbrella trees with branches shade a heart from heat.
But darling, if you ever looked, I was propped against
the sweet one next to me. And while you strolled behind
your savior's path, what could be done when I had broken feet?

There Is the House

There is the house where children used to play
and laughed upon a swing that swung
behind the neighbor's fence.
Was it not the place that held a memory,
of you and I, or maybe only me?

It's pink, that house that holds a banyan tree,
where flooded streets once bled canoes
upon their gravel tops like hungry shores.
A simple place, each number sweetly marked
where station wagons waited—parked.

Abandoned when you left it back in time,
now hollowed eyes, its windows never see.
There's no light that warms the glass,
no gathered drape against the frosty chill
where an entrance beckoned, now it never will.

Oh, how I wish to let that old house know—
the one where all the children used to go,
they'd march around the benched lanai,
blowing horns at bees who lost their wings
from pulling strings through trees. It was I

who lived there very long ago. Pink house,
don't you remember when I slept inside
saying prayers each night until I cried?
Was it not that place that held a memory
of you and I, or maybe only me?

I Swallowed Forty Stars

I swallowed forty stars tonight,
because that's the number the Jews
and Christians assign to everything
according to my Dad, and we're

spending our first New Year's
without my mother, waiting for an epiphany
or message sent by an archangel
telling us she's arrived at her destination—

hopefully bringing her salvation.
So, I figured I might help things out a bit
since there's something magical about
the number forty. Yet, I can't wander

years in the desert or go nights without
water. So I swallowed forty stars;
each one slid down my throat
like fiery ice cream, leaving

blisters in my stomach. When done,
I glanced up and saw her smiling
down
at
me.

An Unexpected Toast

—For the women who came before me

My mother-in-law,
who, in the middle of her stroke,
grinned while she snuck a couple of grapes
off the coffee table, then sprawled
along the celadon sofa like Cleopatra
without the Egyptian gown.

My grandmother,
who danced The Hukilau after returning
from a cruise to the Hawaiian Islands,
wrapped in her flame-retardant grass skirt,
barely moving her hips in figure eights
due to severe arthritis.

My Aunt Ida,
who died from barren nest syndrome
after a lifetime deprived of being
with child, yet gave us everything
imaginable till her heart exploded
from holding too much love.

My mother,
who had the grace of a saint
yet depleted of elegance
through her miserable illness.
Who, while her body was ravaged
by an insufferable disease mustered
enough strength to write in chicken scratch:

This is a wonderful day.

Abandoned

Here's to the tiny jackrabbit
you brought home to me
in your pocket, the one you found
on a day of hunting, the one

you kept warm as it slept inside
your coat pocket on the long drive
back while you listened to the radio
in the old Ford Woodie and smoked

your Chesterfields as you contemplated
life and its complexities between
your rounds of electroshock therapy
and visits to your psychiatrist.

Here's to the love you had for wild
things, the ones you brought home
dead and alive, and that tiny jackrabbit
you cradled in the palm of your hand

as you kneeled beside my childhood
bed, waking me up from a midnight sleep,
two furred ears poking over the corduroy
pouch of your hunting jacket.

Here's to your old Winchester rifle
after a day of hunting; the way you slung
it over your right shoulder like a soldier
searching for battle, and the contentment

it gave you to be alone in the wilderness
with your decoys, bullets, bait-box
and worms, the ones you took with you
on your mornings of wandering

when you roamed the Wetlands in search
of fowl, dead ducks you brought
home and gave to my mother to de-feather
and cook for weekend dinners.

Here's to your laughing and crying
while you sipped a highball sharing
stories of Korea when you were
a warrior, and the conflicted feelings

you had about living and life, long
after the war. Here's to that jackrabbit,
and to all the creatures that survive,
and to all that don't while struggling

to endure unknown obstacles—
to those who are rescued and those
those who die trying, even
if by their own hand.

August Bride

The day she planned my bride's bouquet
our town was pink with streetcar-air
while specks of magic blew through space,
my mother and I were lost somewhere

between gardenias, lace, and pearls,
while garlands braided leafy stems
tight woven wreaths for every face
white orchids sewn along the hems—

and flowered ringlets brushed the gowns
as two by two, they'd walk in rows
along the aisle with petal steps
long streamers tucked in girlish bows—

somehow we felt unmeasured room
through whimsy dreams, we beautified
handpicked within my bride's bouquet,
a perfect life, and then she died.

An Imagined Life

Here, near the grave of the little girl whom I never knew,
but imagine now as I sit down beside her on my visit

to my mother's underground home, and think of her
parents too, her whole family without her now—

her things forever empty, the garden swing
and kitchen table with a vacant chair, a place setting

still there as if she never said goodbye, though
for my own struggles with grief, I imagine her waving

so long, saying how much she'll miss chocolate milk
and ice cream, and how she loved her mother,

and playing hopscotch in the afternoons,
her soft pigtails in the summer sun with glints

of gold woven through braided locks like
dandelions in yellow grass. If I try hard

enough, I can imagine combing her hair
on a day she feels lonely, on a day she misses

the way her mother might have held her tight
as the force of a climbing vine claiming the stucco

of a house. Her mother's arms clinging to her
like leaves of a Virginia creeper, an unstoppable

hold, but for some intervening force, silvered sheers,
or a pruning saw named death. But here near the grave

of that little girl whom I never knew, for a moment—
I almost miss her more than my mother, as I imagine

her undead, dressed up like Cinderella on Halloween
or Amelia Earhart on her way to mark a name across

the sky yet unfound, and just now, as if her little life
has become too big for my imagination, too enormous

to be alone, and as if my mother's life is now too empty,
without her children there to keep her company,

without anyone to need her the way she loved being
needed, I can almost imagine that little girl sitting

on my mother's lap, whispering a secret in her ear—
my mother smiling, as if my mother and that little girl

are no longer lonely, as if I am no longer lonely
either, as if they are enjoying being together,

when, if only for a moment, being in a grave
or above one, is of no perceptible difference.

Acknowledgments

The following poems or some iteration of them have appeared in the journals or publications listed below.

Adelaide: "Before Tomorrow Came"
Cold River Press: "Clemency and the Green House"
Jupiter Review: "Cinders"
Chantarelle's Notebook: "The Boyfriend?"
War Literature and the Arts: "Save Our Souls"
Scapegoat Review: "In the Line at Starbucks"
The Paddock Review: "When You're Small, and Your Father Won't Wake Up"
Feathertail Review: "On the Occasion of Your Mother's Hip Replacement"
Ginosko: "Down by the Watershed," "Epistolary Thoughts from an Aging School Girl," "Minutes from My Doctor's Appt."
Chiron Review: "Negotiations with Things with Plumage"
Wilderness House Literary Review: "After Eating Candy at the Matinee"
Mothers Always Write: "For the Lost Child," "Empty Nester," "Memo to My Children"
Cliterature Anthology: "In Another Life"
Chantarelle's Notebook: "Homage to this Heart"
Ink, Sweat, and Tears: "Regarding Your Submission"
Dreamers Magazine: "Cat Remembers Being Young"
Her Words: "Listen Darling"
The Umbrella Factory: "Evacuation of an Expired Womb"
Sheila-Na-Gig: "Leap Year," "Handful of Stallions at Twilight"
Poets and Artists: "Abandoned"
The Comstock Review: "Audrie's Poem"
Tipton Poetry Journal: "How to Fall in Love with Rober Bly"
Finishing Line Press Chapbook: Object of Desire "Forgive Me," "There is the House," "An Unexpected Toast," "I Swallowed Forty Stars," "August Bride"

Carol Lynn Stevenson Grellas recently graduated from Vermont College of Fine Arts MFA in Writing program, where she received a Merit Scholarship. She is a twelve-time Pushcart Prize nominee and a seven-time Best of the Net nominee. In 2012 she won the Red Ochre Chapbook Contest with her manuscript *Before I Go to Sleep*. In 2018 her book *In the Making of Goodbyes* was nominated for The CLMP Firecracker Award in Poetry, and her poem "A Mall in California" took 2nd place for the Jack Kerouac Poetry Prize. In 2019 her chapbook *An Ode to Hope in the Midst of Pandemonium* was a finalist for the Eric Hoffer Book Award. Her latest collection of poems, *Alice in Ruby Slippers,* was shortlisted for the 2021 Eric Hoffer Grand Prize and awarded an honorable mention in the poetry category. She has served as the Editor-in-Chief for the *Orchards Poetry* and *Tule Review*. Her work has been included in the Saratoga Authors Hall of Fame, and according to family lore, she is a direct descendant of Robert Louis Stevenson.

www.ingramcontent.com/pod-product-compliance
Lightning Source LLC
Chambersburg PA
CBHW020159170426
43199CB00010B/1109